coup de foudre.

ISBN-13: 978-0-578-56458-6
ISBN-10: 0578564580

Front cover design by Desmuir
Book design by Desmuir
Artwork by Desmuir

Self-published by Desmuir in the United States of
America

Printed by Amazon Kindle Direct Publishing

First printing edition 2019

Desmuir
bonjour@jprufrock.com

www.beautifulhypocrisy.com

As we struggle against fragmentation, ambiguity and our continuing existentialism, we find ourselves adrift and connected on relational tables that both juxtapose and polarize the paradox of purpose.

Contents

Forward

I never thought to publish my poetry, but I always wanted to
share them - these verses that reveal and dissemble.
This odd, ambivalent behavior, rife with the cathartic
release of regret and the reconciliation of rigid reason,
drives me mad with introversion and romantic escapism.
The maddening straddle of love and logic in this (post)
wasteland. Would that we don't forget the beauty in our
words and those that wrote them. That we still reach for
the ineffable certain in our inspiration. Finding that
we still wander lonely as a cloud seeking daffodils, and
that the night still walks in beauty. I digress. These days,
Romanticism is rather ephemeral, reflected in these
ofttimes existential poems, and Polonius once said
that brevity is the soul of wit.

love

If I had the agency to make you free.
That we could meet, no longer guilty,
and ease our minds to make amends.
For the times we wavered,
feeble with doubt, that defense
mechanisms, unyielding,
shrouds our minds.

If you had the regency of captious time.
That we could bend, every rigid line,
that delineates this Camelot we found.
For those times we intersected,
ruly locked away, that I abscond
from time, hoping,
to see you smile.

If these days had the urgency of us.
That we could meet, as lovers must,
without the cruelty of parlay.
For these times we miss,
the pith of love, that we weigh
with scales, unassuming,
of one lovely day.

(dharma)

6:00am glances in the
mirror leave me scathed with
thoughts of you.
everyday has been a wraith
to my discretion, and i roll
on to paranoia with the
conviction of your mouth
to mine.

we can ask the world what this is.
the neurosis of loving
when we had no business of doing so.
no more rovings and meetings –
the makings of severance.

intolerance was ever free.
tell me, did you leave your
promises by the tree where we laid
and dallied for the months that
were never to be?

i am back from the dead –
west of eden on a side of paradise
that this hub of urban rock
praises to no end. i am bending
my pretenses to suit you instead
of ending the charade that is us.
lust made its cue, went askew and fell
in constellation drops on you and the
few breaths drawn in lieu of our silhouetting
in this metropolitan view.

hold the moon and cry to the dawn –
sleepless yawns over the lawn
of bygone memories in the clouded
song of the morning.

never leave but stay only a while.
tiles of habitual self-mockery
makes me tense for your love and
takes the relief from my
tapered sighs – every line that found

a minute on the strand of our lost
smiles.

it is still a wasteland where we play
and hate our hampered humanity humming
humbly in our homes. it creeps. it leaps.
it is the last of my taunting.
it must be me pretending to be
free.

just remember in december when
i encumber you with touches sombre
that i wondered if we could
ever be.

(love letter)

If I took a little time –
selfishly for my own
To do what hearts like mine
are prone to do when every line
traces itself to you.

A bit of time to breathe –
suddenly on my own.
To know this breath of mine,
slow and sure, is a quantum
entangled with yours.

As if for the first time –
Achingly new. Deliberately unknown.
To brave this world of ours,
spinning callously amongst the stars,
together with you...

Good evening, Love.

(sleep learning)

If you please, an enduring lease.
Bits of you, all of me.
Context rather than personality.
The consensus of identity.
In absentia, the thought inuring.
That is our play, a yes to dreaming.
When awake I no longer see you.
When sleeping I held you.
We cannot be.
This tragic dramaturgy.
A pursuit never ending.
The lessor of our intent in default
of our pedigree. Our dive
so easy into that our
murmurs pledge unheeding.
Your navel to my brow leaves
etches of a mandarin complex.
A sense too tense, a lapse of
a sensibility wise to malcontent.
Still unravished. Quiet in this
chase where my lines repent.
My fleeing muse.
Am I almost to you?
To that beautiful closing
we muse?
Stay your steps. Turn my way.
These irises. When they
find yours in an intimacy
too binding to break,
then will I know
compulsion to this
instant ever.
Know this is
certainly true.
When, at last, I am
faced with you.

(ode)

moving through the spell of time.
i'm ensnared.
confused.
not wearing my jacket of rhyme
so well.
please tell the midnight to come
of what to bring to my sleep.
a moment with you
without the walls.
frigid with heat
in the evening calls.
i breathe quickly.
thinking of the possibility.
the dream of us
in the slow champak ardor
of what we seize.
the circle and ring
of our infinity.
the forever hills
where we may sing.
everything has an ending
yet i sleep the dream
of beginning.

(cypress)

Having rarely looked when the sky held you.
With the stars aligned on that cosmic pew.
Rushing I fell. In getting up, I rue.
That heliotropism was all I knew.

The shades we mistrust. The past we peruse.
Those moments, like an odd glamour miscued,
Is my obstinate wall lowered. Confused.
This lunacy that a full moon imbues.

Our lives in tandem, our hushed breaths subdued.
The lives we nurture, the hopes we pursue.
All coalesce, unhindered, in this view.
Longing for this half moon I never knew.

(demi lune)

If only for a moment
that I would love you
more than my life itself,
then that would be
a moment to live
as if love were my life.

If only for a spell
that you would gaze
upon me as though
enraptured by the
moment I cast my
gaze in thrall to yours.

These skies of Taipei
in diurnal contradiction
to the falling tides,
crestfallen and heavy,
on the morning
shores of my soul.
I do not want to go.
Those pastures that
await me back home.
I do not want to go.
to that which is
familiar and known.
I do not want to go.
To my old life
content but alone.
Rather would I be
in your arms on
this isle Formosa.
That this moment from
The center sever.
That this spell bind
this world ever.
That once bound
is immutable as stone.
If only for a moment.

(salt field poet)

it has always been you.

every time i feel myself falling.
every time i remember to be me.
the world is passing, and we are seen
in those moments when the
night is still in her infancy.

She, too, knows that it is you.
She knows of the ache, the pining,
and the keening.

it is still you.

i still wonder - often into the night.
i still find the restless chill of my
brow an old delight not worth
playing to.
pretending was never my
want or need
nor was pleading or
laughing untrue.

the night still mocks my
soul, and I will have you know
that I was always so.

always thinking of the idea of us.

the impalpable smiles that hold your face
make my youth simplicity's grace.
i am fallen from the cliff.
only half a man at times.
lift me, love, and forever know
that i have grown as much as i can
without you….

that i wish to grow old with you.

(hemlock st)

These spots of time.
Like wine in my glass.
Holding that last incline
as pouring, sipping, you
spilled your eyes
upon mine.
Line for line, you remind
me of me.
At least we are free.
No sign of that
uneasy feeling when
meeting someone
strangely like me.
No, tell me your
heart is as rampant
as ever.
Yes, take my breather.
Eager to keep our
pulse going.
That easy smile
of yours ever coupled
with mine in October.
This timeline is skewed.
Like a wreck of a train
you and I boarded.
In good faith we trusted.
In love we lusted for
that we could only
find in dreams that
curled around your lips
smiling in uncertainty
as I am writ from you.
Mind urging.
Body tugging.
Soul so taken
with you.
This freedom in writing.
This joy in being.
This fear in your eye
a wistful imagination
of mine.
Will such things in

time, sluggish and prudent,
be just another line?
When you and I drenched
the evening sky.

(cape verde)

Grant me bliss before morning come.
In lulling tunes by twilight strum.
The deepness of my heart revealed
In traveling dreams half-hidden.
Moonlight ray on my lips hum
The melodies by my pride concealed.
These sounds of desire spring unbidden
To dance my thoughts with erotic drum.

Night's breathing of enchanted sleep
Whispers your name in my slumber deep.
The old scents my senses assail
Upon this moment of midnight reprise.
Forgotten cravings over my body creep.
In its passage, my yearnings trail.
These phantoms of night, so clever their guise.
To invoke your face with the hope I keep.

The trees without to my prayers sway.
Falling winds among the maples play.
The passing of their tussle my breath,
So short, so quick - my dream may fade.
'Wake me not!' I fervently pray.
Let sleep be unto timeless death.
Taken for my beloved's sake.
Denied ever to tedious day.

(arabian serenade)

Your heart is your home as much as my own.
Somewhat dilapidated - somehow still standing.
The old columns, in hardening, now crumble as if letting go.
The chateau a surviving testament of our will.
These homes of ours were numb - silent in the wind.
The hearths witness to what we had to brace ourselves from.
Bitterness in the main hall.
Jealousy in the cellars.
Disappointment and embarrassment hid in the attic.
Those bedroom doors that locked the heart break
away from the love we shared in the foyer.
Somehow these things can still be felt.
Humming away in this house of former Gables -
These hearts and homes of ours.
Something has been amiss.
Most often in the night, the stars hold us.
Kiss us with cool, silver tides of remedy bound
by sweet words that loosen the locks we set on the door.
Mostly during the day, the sunlight highlights the decay -
the garish paint peeling away from the sultry wood.
The wood that held our homes together.
The spirit that held the strength to rebuild -
to grow as though our roots were our souls and latched
to the land.
These homes of ours that still stand.
We restored the halls so that laughter would echo again.
We opened the cellars so that we could share wine again.
We cleared the attic so that the noon sun could enter again.
We embraced the possibility that our hearts could break again.
That all we needed was for the other to fill the space
in our once empty homes.

(posterity)

daydreaming i missed you.
wanted to tell you about these skies that flutter
when you and i are away from the other.
i shiver. muttering thoughts moving
ponderously from the center.
if ever i forgo the usual.
if ever i was hopeful.
know it is you i hold
this sky for.

deep in this spell we fell up.
bits of perception. an adjunct angle of view.
every turn that breaks from what we are used to.
what you used to be used to.
what i may not be used to.
as if our minds unbalanced by a bit.
as if our wills were misfit.
this binary disposition of mine.
that hexing grin of yours.
these engaging days of ours
like memoirs in a golden bottle
cast into space to fall
back into deep waters.

i thought i lost you.
tides in my eyes.
the swells that rise
and bring me closer.
you ground me.
running your fingers
across my demeanor.
i hold you closer.
this current that binds us.
this land charmed
by our endeavor
if ever there was an ever.

if ever lovers err.
your hand in mine.
we can do this.
let us swim for
those farther shores
of deep learning.
your hand in mine.
daydreaming i missed you.

(dishabituation)

There had to be you
In this tract I swallow through.
This moment after that I
savor and resent.
Those times before we spy
with instruments meant for
dissent.
On this pond. This small body
that I try.
This last time I pen in
hopes to find you again.
The beginning of another strand.
Another skit. And I still
think of us in a land
where our home may stand.

(recourse)

Look to the sea, my love.
See you not its vast dispassion?
Look to the cliffs which hang over.
Do they gather the waves that crash on?
Have you any inkling, my dear,
Of the purpose of seabird flight?
Have you seen many horizons
O'er the silver of dark water at night?
Hear you not the rocky grumble
Of dreamy sleep in the depths?
Its gentle echo resound and heard
In private nooks and secret clefts.
Do sea serpents rear great necks
Or mermaids in these waves swim?
Does the antique mystery of deep waters
Persist in midnight dreams of men?
Look again, beloved, and wonder.
Is this corner of earth too calm?
Here you are in my embrace.
So held you will not see harm.
Together we stand, gazing at the sea.
Lips that mumble suddenly still.
Let me draw you closer to me.
Our yearning hearts each other will fill.
But the sea!… The sea is dully dead.
Its body at content rest.
Neptune will not raise his ire
To pound these shores will zeal and zest.
But hark!… See the darkening skyline?
Are those clouds like wind to mast?
What strange breaks in monotony.
O' my sweet!… The sea is alive at last.

(cliff perching)

We lay among the willows.
The August sun upon your skin.
Pleasant brown earth a downy pillow.
The breath of our bodies a sin.

You rose admidst the fields.
Venus born of the land.
I shudder - my soul to yours yields.
I implore - stay where you stand.

Stay not forever, just awhile.
If I may be so bold asking.
Let not fade that gentle smile
'Til the moon upon us night bring.

Under the stars may we talk
Of easy pleasures times from hence.
Then among the maples may we walk
To pass the night in innocence.

Love but once, not twice.
The postmodern creed.
One taste may suffice
All desire and need.

So went the brief night.
In careless slumber I knew
The passing breeze of your flight
And how cold this heart grew.

The river willows now weep.
In grief though not for me.
For the fields that keep
The memory of what could not be.

(among the willows)

i only walk these shoes
for a glimpse of you
in the hanging shades of
this life.

one moment where i
may, if i may,
see some destination.
some harbor
far from my origination.
just once i'd like to see
you see me.
for what i am.
unbroken but seeking
to be whole.
then hold me as i you.
i only walk these shoes

(a mile)

I had a dream of us
in some dystopia.
Far flung.
These scenes and scapes
with you and me.
Yet so close
I can touch the brooding
frown upon your face.
So still I chase
this dream
until waking it seems
I can only hold on
a short moment
where a multitude of meaning
taxes and escapes my
half waking abstract.
Your smile.
Your laugh.
Your release
of my honor.
Was it only that?
That act meant
to play out in
the brief entwining
between us.
I could not sleep,
and when I did
it was to unmake you.
In every waking moment,
a reminder of you to
embrace in bitter
bliss I knew.
I will leave
with you.
Into that soft
goodnight we
always spoke of.
Into that gentle
evening full of
promise.
Full of us.
Were we just

in our younger years?
Where we could
claim you and I
with reprise.
Over and over
again.
That thorny halo
upon your brow
pricks at the
trapped zeal
of my mind
that finds yours
soon enough.
Pursuing our quarry.
On this surreal journey.
In this I have
found truth.
Only to lose you
to the dawn
sighing succinctly -
quick in its urgency
when breaking the
fast of my ardor.
Reminding me of
the temperament
of your affectation.
I should have been true
instead of the wastrel
of intent that left us rent,
jaded and spent.
Now we both
trudge with hearts
too heavy to bear.
With souls walled
too high to clear.
I wish these
lessons in love
would not scorn me so.
I wish I could leave
a bit of myself in
a spot of color
that catches your eye.

In the moist scent of
dew as you inhale
the morning air.
In the lay of the
nightingale thrush
keeping these rustic lands.
In the subtle mote of lime
colluding secretly
in your sangria.
In the brush of felt
on your velour robe
as you wrap
yourself goodnight.
As we slip and
sever our ties
in this dystopia
where I loved
you at
first sight.

(Marlowe & More)

sitting across from you.
velvet between us.

thrusting through the feathered fold
i am cold. emotionally myopic
i am told.
shaved ice. soft and not yet old
has slid down forming
our union.

the brim of my cup steals my smile.
the eyes - bewildered by caffeine, domesticated by
cream;
teems and leaps at the hush of your surprise.

be with me.

can we be?

five years of this and i
find that i might forget
if you do not see
the idea of us…the notion of
trust.

breathe.

sidewalk cafes always predicate
situations like this and i
feel the pedestrian
rhythm of your breath
saddling my own.

(can we be?)

My footsteps were heavy.
A child to the rain falling.
I should have stepped lightly
now that you are falling.
In dead space, you were floating.
Moondust suspended in time.
Knowing was a painful thing.
Slipping sometimes when you climb
that arduous path back up.
The witchery that keeps you down.
Hovering silently above
an ocean where you may drown.
Earth bound, entropic
entry into our terrestrial maze.
When our days were spent in caves.
That your star, in rising, blaze.
To break this inert latitude of space.

(ancient astronaut)

I saw me in you.
Catching moon rays in lieu
of golden days ripened with
the passion of night to lay.
I live a dream like you.
That a home could be crafted
by our hands with wood hewn
from this land long slumbering.
Waiting beneath our bare feet
on the grass where the
drowsy air has drafted.
I glance over at you.
Seeing the joining of
feelings that leaves my
breath captured yet not empty.
A reminder that I have yet
to truly touch you if only
you would let me.
I rise with you.
Slowly like the sun hitched
by the yoke of the evening
no longer daunted by
past misgivings.
Quickening as my
pulse gets when
stumbling
I fall for you.

(cape verde revisited)

Again it was in my thoughts.
The admission of ambivalence.
Evidence of nostalgia.

Again it plied my thoughts.
The persuasion of kiss.
The scent of our afterglow.
The butterfly of our encapsulation
Flitting away on fey wings.
That need entwines our souls
Makes beautiful hypocrisy.
The restlessness of memory:
Your calves inclined with
The closing of the bedroom door.

Again it was in my thoughts.
The shallowness of it all.
The ennui of forgetting.

(cocoon)

the clown

who's that?

prattling on the silver shore… paddling my
aquatic whore… the wind may play a sultry
mix… spin like veils 7 times removed from
licked lips… if only they would ease my
broken harp… strung like carcasses upon the
door

~

you mock… lock… stock… load…… shoot……
white rum over your silly, presbyterian
dress…… elmer's glue in between the
toes…… have you a hankerchief,
dear?… silly me… let me reload

~

as it was meant to be… tygers and lambs and
cosmic trees… collision forbode and
separation fortold……what's right and
wrong, vintage and old… i have been sold
long before this…… the service of madness…
reckless with science… this sample
space of us… if wishes flew on wings of dust…
august ashes swirling a tempest …

~

akimbo paradoxes like you and me…
dawn and dusk…
standing high when the sun hung
low…
between you and me…
each on the other's whisper…
and I knew as we flew…
drawn to flesh.

gouged by our syncopation...
abruptly... fallen... pull down
the shade so we may lay
besides our dismay.

~

most days are like monday.
slow and gray - in stone we lay.
fingernails on the
underside of our boat to hell, but oh well.
wish me well, my clown.
we cannot sell the vibrance of intent to the crowd.
shrouded as we are. lauded for our speech.
let us teach the folly and hypocrisy.
then, perhaps, we would not wish for death so keenly...

(to candy clowns)

on 12/8/2000 she wrote:

From: "Bob Inurelap"
To: brandedblue@hotmail.com
Subject: "Love..love will keep us together.."
Date: Fri, 08 Dec 2000 22:38:22 -0000

Hi..my name is Tsui Monkey and I'm an alcoholic. It
started at birth. My momma monkey, left my daddy for
a big gorilla. I was then tossed about from palm tree
to palm tree. I eeked out a miserable existence in the
forest. Eating from furry hand to furry mouth. I was
beat up and abused for years by a gang of rabid,homo-
sexual chimps. I ran away to the city, where I lost
myself. Alone, I found myself in bars. Lonely, hairy
and flea ridden. I began drinking heavily. Turning to
female street performing monkey girls. You know..the ones
that do it for money. I found a job with the circus.
It was there that I found salvation. The answer to
all my prayers.I was riding a bike..while standing on my
head. She was wearing a big red nose. Red curly wig.
The most beautiful clown I have ever seen in my life.
I was instantly smitten, bitten by a love bug with
fangs. After our act, we would meet, late at night.
Behind the elephant cages. And while the smell was
overbearing..it had little effect on us. Steamy nights
in the hay..over and over. Our love grew like wild
weeds and dandelions..high and plentiful. She would
whisper sweet nothings in my ear..and I, oh I would
spout verse. Our souls..salsa danced. Our passion..was
like a Ricky Martin video born to life. I asked for her
hand one hot, smelly night..and she said yes. It was
the happiest day in my life..the
happiest night. We kissed as one. Monkey and clown. I
heard Captain and Tennille playing in my mind..I heard
Lionel Ritchie, and Celine Dion. The next day. Oh god.
The next day. It was a normal routine. My clown was on
the high wire. She was tightrope walking..like she'd
done a million times before. She was so beautiful.
Those shoes..that hair. She looked over and smiled at

36

me..I was driving a little car. It was then I saw
her lose her balance. She teetered..back and forth
for a second and than fell.. like a 100 pound sack of
bricks. She fell until she couldn't fall anymore. Until
she was a flat..red..stain on the earthen floor of the
big tent. I cried that night..I cried, and drank. I
drank myself into oblivion. I was fired from the circus.
I wandered aimlessly on the streets. I drank myself into
the hospital. I missed my clown so much I didn't want
to live. In the hospital I met a psychiatrist. He ran
many tests on me. Including the Rorschach test..and
I saw her. A red ink spot on the white flash card..MY
CLOWN. It was then I knew..I needed to change..I needed
to get better….that night in my sleep, I heard it..
The Captain and Tennille..singing. I knew it was her,
and I knew what I had to do..

My name is Tsui Monkey..and I'm an alcoholic...[1]

... and I replied:

red inkblots on the card make remarkable
scenery.
it is unnecessary beauty on top of beautiful
abstraction.
i found her in the miasma of psychiatric
interpretation.
the clown.
the silly clown.
blotting out my sanity.

i was in the Thurber carnival.
it was daunting, alien... carnal.
nights at the circus were
never like this.
without remiss in the burlesque.
there was no hope
that it would ever end.
asphyxiation from
hyperbole threatened at
every bend – sending
suffocation from
three rings.
there she was.
prancing about singing
the harlequin chant
in the cacophony of air horns.
i saw this mordantly:
the smudge of mascara,
the caustic red of her lips,
the well formed bridge of her nose
under the circus cherry.
she swayed a seven veiled dance
in caricature shoes.
i felt myself rising at
something that should
have made me wince
in the womb.

my sense of the world
was less firm than ever·

a tomb of viscera
that choked my resolve
to breathe.

……yes.

"So what do you see?", my psychiatrist
whispered.

"A kidney…that's all."

I could breathe again.

(love will keep us together)

It was very likely true.
Being mad about you.
But you are just that.
And very likely more.
Those brazen days you and I
sculpted the sky from the
whispers between our lips.
These dreams of you and I
slipping free of the venus
bound in between your hips.
The fury of desire only
cooled by the embrace of
your thighs.
I was not mad at you.
Just that you confound me.
Enveloped in confusion.
As I find clarity in coming.
You are so very likely.
Fuck you.

(likely me)

save me. it is all you can do.
when the last of the lines are off
the glass we fall to sleep
like cherubs from the sun –
dimming our way through
the atmosphere.

your smile was ethereal
in my hazy and haughty
heaven, and I tried to fly
just above your wings
so I could see you skimming
the tapestry of earth
like my breath over your
bright shoulders.

we are getting older.
wiser.
waning.
wanting.
wishing that our sleep
was no necessity.
the white snow capped on
your visage is mirage and
mirrors my fancy…..
mocks my memory.

you were beautiful. I
always knew, but I could not
touch you until now.

until we both fell from
our long flight like abandoned
creatures in a wasteland, and I cried
for your help.

(king's habit)

here is the void.
a choice cut of misery.
fallen you and chanced on me.

ever see the unseen dance naked on your table?

unstable me and dizzy you.
like angels at the bar.
far and few in between...

your thighs sizing up
my entry.
dipping into you
was frozen fear
of my own
soul.

don't you know?
we grow on fancies
and pretend fallacies –
denying the world of
our precious precociousness.

we knew long before.
before the fall.
before the slip.
before lips like ours
found the other.

look for me, love.
find me and let
me know that i can
breathe again.

(old souls)

grasping at seams.
stitches that mean nothing
when i save them.
a rag and rhyme
that hitches my disarray.

fey, love, just fey.
the lining on your
stocking makes
a silver canteen
of me.
i yearn to press my
wit…. .

my wit, that is…
let me whip out my wit..

to press against your hip.
let it stay there.
soothed by your discretion.
the indiscreet tuning of
your mind.
let it stay there
until it gyrates.
until we inundate the
wellspring of who we are
with sleeping pills
and whispers goodnight.

(introvert)

It's blue like the moon in my sultan seas,
and I float and gloat on memories of thee
in trees with bees about your knees.

Aphrodite of my tongue - seashells if you please.
Rising from the ocean - tang on your breath. What's
left in the musty dialogue between our souls?

If what was and what might be were any
indication of this then we could be free in the ever
flowing words in the old molds of cold rhymes and
stanza folds.

What made me do this?
What makes you tick?

If I could but touch that one place where we meet then
I might not be so crazed at the very thought of going
back - back to the delays and forays and neurasthenics
that drive me from sleep and keens at your every turn.

I burned our pictures, tore the
core of our keepsakes and let
the ash flake into nothing
on the rug of our mistake.

I would like nothing more than to quit. Sit like a
catatonic on the edge of dull wit. Flit in the stream
of my inward river of affirmation kits and meet you by
the broken curbs of dim lit minds. I laugh. We often
laugh at situations like this. Without remiss and
without recourse.

Think again, love.

Of course, I am free.

(monrovia)

acropolis.
high and fortified.
i make my way through the milling of the
city proper.

stiletto jabs on the pavement.
what marked lines
that shoes define.
you mocked me on the corner
with the small of your back
pressed against the wind.
you and i rubbing the 3 feet of
meta space between us.

only briefly.

properly.

friction cupped by a neurotic hand.

it seems i do this every morning
on my way to the parthenon.

...and the fall of sharp heels
drag that thought way behind
the round small of my head and neck.

you and i passing.
like ancient metropolitans in the
morning cast of drones.

(dtla)

You and I are akin.
Deep within my fettered whims.
All over again -
your eyes on mine and lost time.
Nothing forebode this from the first
time we met. Nothing means this
when we fall to forget
in each's arms like sunset.
Like nothing I have felt
in all these years. I cannot bear
the thought of this.
Another red consumed by flame
and names and faces called by blame.
Sadness smells of smoke
and look at us now - no longer smiling,
no longer enamoured by something new.
Old before our time. Trapped in
the old ways that trend the young
lives we live. I am so sorry.

I would bleed as I have done many
times before from need.
Let out the passions and angst
that makes me the man I am.
A river of red like the endless
miasma muzzling my grief.
If we could walk the earth like
children and make ourselves free.
But, no. We talk of Saturn
in Jupiter's phase and daze
the last of sunlight
with Märzen and grammar fit for
our grandparents.
If our sighs were any indication of the
designs of our intention then we
could embrace with your face to mine.
Spreading softly for the umber
shade of my disposition.
The anarchy of our decision.

And all the while we
wait for something that may
never come, that may never be in
the decadent rules of my denial
and diffidence. I feel short of breath,
and the bob of your hair is death
to my need to be generic like
some player in Passos's parallel
Uneasy like the flapper manual
in your easy hands.
I can almost trip and fall to the floor
with hands clasped to a god I never
trusted. If I could see you
again in the salt and searing
blear of my guilt, I would tell
you that I wished we were stars in
a constellation full of idyllic fields
that held nothing but the fruit of
our cosmic assembly.

Nothing ever held me
long or consistently.
I could never sell the
parts of me that were
the most desireable. It falls
to you to make me pliable
in the rigidness of
who I chose to be.
If you could see what
I wished we could.
The stars and the old hills
still untouched.
The last of Lucy's shade in
flowers by ancient cottage doors.
And what for?
We only see the sudden catch
of iconoclasts like us.
Though we do nothing for change,
we change everything.

(kindred)

O' Poet with soldier sword
And duty to soul adorned.
Of plays whom thou art lord
But yet thy features scorned.

A gentle soul so well hid
By attitude hard and manners aloft.
Were that veneer cast and rid,
T'would reveal a heart most soft.

Poor Monsieur De Bergerac.
What a jest indeed.
Of honour, thou dost not lack.
A loving heart thou dost not need.

Whom dost thou love?
Worthy of thy verse.
A maid the rest above
With beauty thee must curse.

Roxanne the fair:
The beauteous rose.
Her soul thy care.
Her mind thou hast chose.

Thee, that women most plain
Would mock and despise
Would prefer to bear the pain
Of loving a hopeless prize.

Love her not, Bergerac!
Make in truth, not feign,
The friendship act,
And sane thy will remain.

Dost Roxanne not view
Thyself as worthy and true?
Platonic glances are so few;
Be satisfied with thus in lieu.

Yet Roxanne to thee appeal
To win another's heart.
Thine will to hers kneel,
As thy soul wrenches apart.

de Neuvillette:
The dashing youth.
With eyes in blue set-
A soldier most couth.

'Tis he Roxanne adores.
The bewildered man.
'Tis he, as well, implores
Your aid to win Roxanne.

The love thou may uphold-
From thy breast unending spring.
Would not make thee so bold
As to refuse her gentle asking.

With laden mind, thou must embark
To make de Neuvillette shine.
Under guise, in cover of dark;
Roxanne thou wooed with words divine.

Thou hast achieved thy goal.
Roxanne now de Neuvillette's sweet.
At what cost? Thee only knows.
Her love only in dreams to greet.

So forlorn. To life despair.
A tear to past and misery shed.
When wings of war fly the air-
Now to death seek thee to wed.

de Neuvillette rides thy side
To clash arms 'gainst foe.
There he falls to reaper's tide.
His death Roxanne's woe.

With final breath so weak,
He did ruefully admit.
The silent denials of heart speak:
Roxanne loved more thy charm and wit.

Then away he passed
To upper planes and fields unknown.
How pitifully Roxanne wept alas.
Her sorrow a mirror to thine own.

The years have turned
With hopes waiting to be.
Fourteen summers have burned,
Yet still she knows not thee.

Love unrequited. Silence its ward.
Long nights hast thou slept,
Thy hand on restless sword.
Longer days with thy secret kept.

Thine enemies conceive a plot
To finally cast thee down.
Your subtle wish at last begot.
The bells knell a bitter sound.

Delirious thou stumbles blind
To seek and find dear Roxanne.
The inflicted wound clouds thy mind
To clutch at breast with shaking hand.

Thou finds her in serene church.
Her visage the same as past.
She looks up to thy painful lurch,
And holds thy falling body fast.

There upon her bosom in locket lay
The letter of thine own hand.
Without a glance thou recites away,
Word for word, thy heart's demand.

Impending darkness maliciously cloaks
The final vision of thy lovely sweet.
If her eyes thee saw and sobbing choke,
Mayhap angels thou wouldst regret to meet.

Roxanne does love at end.
Thy soul does she realize.
Thine spirit will never bend,
Thy love in her heart now lies.

Thus thee so dramatically dies.
In the arms of thy life's love.
Laughing softly when thee flies
Into the embrace of heaven above.

(ferrer)

There is damsel distress on your dress.
The train is coming, and I am taller.
Growing bold as should every bard
coming of age on
metropolitan grounds.
It sounds and knells
what delphi fortells:

so Oedipus, his brood and us
are blind and bound to masquerade as such.

Pacific pacification and
Transcontinental transcendence
bearing down on us.

I can feel the earth rumbling
in the fold of the horizon –
a mechanical, urban beast ready to devour.
I can feel the coils taking
too long to spring (too trivial) – on course.

All magic is tragic.
A thaumaturge would know.
A sigh escapes me.
A tongue warped by wisdom.

I have to let you go.

A villain is laughing somewhere
and the train is on the go.
I should unbind you for
the conservatists and the droll.

No miracles today. I could not save you,
because I let you go.

(antigone)

Things like you matter when people like me
exist.
Is it a thing that makes time?
A time to make a thing?

Freedom is forbidden when we cry like draconian
lovers.
Hurt like martyrs kissing the children of
others.

Look at me.

Far fetched.
Far from freedom.
Far into the night that freezes me alive.
Far gone.
Far too much into this.

I see you in strange moments.

You are beautiful,
And I am wicked to say so.

(things like you)

they came upon the evening
too late.
hands held in the lamppost light.

a line had formed·
melding with the side
of the building.

willing themselves on,
they grabbed the tail.
victim to the whole.

almost.

the stale shade of winter
made them swoon.
too soon into the night.
too early for the tuxedo
black and trite.
too gaudy was
her gown.

much to our delight.
we mocked them in the banality
of our scorn.
we locked them in unseen
cages and threw the key
to the mob.
we stocked our cellars with
cruelty and dispensed
our wine for laughter.

our smirks made us divine.
we could judge the crime
of originality in
our world matted in gray.
we knew they were not
to be like us,
and we loved our
industries and made
effigies of them.

they were no longer at the end
of the line.
they were part of the draconian body.
they laughed to each other.
they covered the other's face with kisses.
they left and moved away.

the line healed itself.
stitched by the constituency
of conviction -
of intentional fallacy.

we made demons of the
shadows cast by they
who left.
must it be right and just?
they were almost whores
like us.

(we are they)

dear sky,

i slept last night flying through you. smiling
slightly and flocking a flight of thoughts too much to
hold. so bold the notion of skimming this ocean would
make these weary wings fly to write such verse this
morning.

gliding quickly in a world shifting and thinking of
us in a union uplifting. seeming soaring this ideal
roaring the voices from my breathing whisper. this no
journey of careless yearning that any man as i should
blindly venture.

ever me and such as you could shake the center from
such cold winter. into spring we laughing sing and
hope eternal for our summer. would this be real in
falling prayer we kneel with hymns made to keep us
forever?

please, if you will, heed us well the moments still
made to come whenever. tell me yet the clouds to haze
the last of our fell weather will demand that clever
words are needed never. in disarray my words will ever
be full of feeling for you i'd rather.

should i fail and questing trail behind the stars i
implore might snicker. too many sighs to match. too
much would flicker yet still i hope to meet in your
eyes the spark that inspires wonder.

hills too green and rocks too hard may cut our vision
asunder. from your full kiss and arms around would i
cherish a sweet reminder of what might be us entwined
in slumber. from this now, my lovely sky, would you
know my answer?

(arlington)

i didn't sleep well last night without your morning
kiss to greet me as i seek the cold air outside the
covers. whatever the mood could have been better with
you to strum my slant eyed waking with the hum of your
lips i can never graze too soon.

if not for the thought of hills almost too green and
left unseen for the while we styled our embraces after
races from the valley dream. almost seeming too
unreal, i feel the creek speak to me cheek to your
cheek and the waters rush unchecked to the court of
our yard overlooked by the balcony.

would you mock the current of my thought often sparked
by the incandescent filament never spent or stocked by
any but me as it is true just for you? too many
restless days fall into play in the brooding of the
past at last, and bring that soothing breath that i
breathe today.

lovers stay wicked with the spite of spurn. grind
their roots and pale away under the falling sticks of
sentinel trees that seize the last of their envious
tricks and overshadow the last of what they may.

under the noon of such a boon, our garden takes life
raking the dead dirt into being where once ill will
lurked and now lies too vicious to unearth. just in
time, roses bloom and assume colors too wild, too soon
and i am near stricken with visions of me in black and
white on you.

i miss you so and with a heart beating innocent,
young and true. if ever i endeavored, it was for you
in lines and stanzas i always knew when stammered for
sooth. come to me and i to you. could you smell the
love i brew?

(märzen)

Amidst the fallen words that
lie between us,
Your dry lips pick through
the old remedies.
The panacea soaked in blood.
The skit of your skirt,
The upward turn of your bust –
Indemnities
Against my back moving farther
away from you.

Drifting was ever the style.
Moving through you ever so
lovely in design.
Silver watches and
vintage wine.

All I ever wanted to do
was share the sky
with you for a while.

You speak of trenches
and winters
in the steadfastness of
our summer.
When lines and love
was our little urban
renaissance.

The mirror and glass
that made follies of
our attempts at
pedestrianism.

We were both
too unhappy for that.
You were playing the ingénue
with hardly a clue
about me.

About sangria, peacock plumes,
and vanity.

Pride aside,
I hope you never share
the sky with anyone
else.

Bye.

(metropolitan)

like an old boulder,
a dusty mantle,
tarnished silver,
played out metaphors,
well worn similes,
proverbs partial to partisanship,
phrases plied for platitudes,
and then there is me.

like earth rising,
I grope through the strata.
earthly layers of my epidermal flesh.

I count down to my final blessing in random
order.

seven. vanity. I smile for hidden eyes.

six. envy. I seek to be a philistine.

five. gluttony. I would indulge exuberance
herself.

two. sloth. probably why I am already on two.

one. you. how else would there be this at all?

silence. slow, sweet silence for my soliloquy.

I rhyme therefore iambic...

I smile as should you.

(do tell)

my clown is lovely when she is cracked...
tightroped and lipped to
shear her own lungs...
my clown is lovely when she is cracked...
caustic and constrained to her own tongue.

my clown is fallen and away.
she is cracked.
she is bleeding.
she is in the carnival eye.

the ringmaster's whore that i adore.
she is far and away.
clown makeup so fae and fey-
a tear streaking as it may.

spectate. see her?
inside the ring - the hub of her thing.
my clown is so adorable when
she is
cracked.

(circus nights)

strands

Aloe caresses fall on her skin.
The dermatology of mythology.
Midway down her length,
Iridescence scales my eye.
Maritime and so sublime.
Bring me to the waters.

She was climbing like a phantom.
Trapped in something unlike altitude.
She could not breathe or voice.
Her hair and neck moist.
I was crying to see her like so.

A shrine was waiting for the old world
chemistry.
The alchemy to make her like me-
Foolish and proud
And eager for death by sophistry.
We were all lied to.
Her most of all.
Enthralled by love.
Now I was just afraid -
Deathly scared of dying too early or of
Natural causes.
All my doing would not be mine.
All that should have been mine might not be.

Faltering. Flailing. Fucking my psyche.

She drank the last of the blue,
Took the final due from my
lips.

Drowning and dying in our air.

(daughters of the air)

I resented you a bit.
Leaving as you did.
I faltered a bit.
Remnants that once hid.
The irony of proximity
with your face to mine
is hard to breach.
This almost treatise
between us teases
at what could be.

What once I drew from.
Numb with years.
What once you grew from.
Sums my fears.
The needless pageantry
of reasoning.
I want you.
But you may
not see that
as possibility.

You resented me a bit.
Watching you walk amid
the midnight motes
swaying a bit under
the moonless grid
of our parting.
I think of you.
With the hope
of impossibility.
I resented you a bit.

(tacit)

Your chair across the dining
table sat empty.
A reminder that our hearts, like
my appetite, was arbitrary.
These days of ours, given to fancy,
cast over and through the net, like
currency virtualized for the sake of economy.

Saying I missed you would be faux pas.
In the sense that we all have forgotten art.
The old gods have fallen.
Something, in living today, we knew.
Our inbox, relentlessly, keeps calling.
The likes, and dislikes, we eschew.
That, in living, we embolden.

Surely, my kind is dying if not dead.
My pen, in strokes like recursive computing,
is extant in metaphor only.
When we lament our missed meetings
as if our attempts at trying, an atavus
rising - gave meaning to entwining.
Booting the need from which we were bred.

(canto)

That was a foolish notion I
Had entertained and memory
Will haunt beyond this childhood cry.
That I had raced with symmetry
Of soul and mind both tightly fused.
As one they raced with pounding heart
For beauty uncompared I mused.
To summon thought of her was art
And praises of that thought a hymn.
Love bordering idolatry.
Yet I to her was just a whim.
Now knowing in tranquility.
So scorned and mocked by vanity.
Her name no longer litany.

(Araby)

Those quiet trees in our range murmur
a lament to those requiems we utter
when passing solemnly under the
shade cast by our favorite maple.
Remembering the spring we shared
by the brook where we cast stones
too light with our laughter into
the ponds of our copse easy with
the smiles of summer's ripples.
Your dappled coat. My wool scarf.
Those accoutrements we saved for fall.
That we might, to playfully spite,
the bronze days before old man's winter.
Frosting the air between us with
the breath of shared desire.
A longing for ever.
And when again I walk this glen,
I swear I live the moment with you as then.

(psalm)

I tried to forget all about you.
Your steps traced on synaptic seams
pick stitched by what seems to be
memories of you.
It was neural yet static.
The cleft the same but a leap erratic
These hurdles in my head
a lonesome goal to you.
I am iota.
Struggling to cross the membrane
bound in regret of you.
To escape into inhibition
that I might, excited and frantic,
be pruned into insensate reflection of you.
I am through.
Charging in a flood of change
rushing away from you.
To find a state free and easy.
A place torpid - no longer pedantic.
I tried to forget all about you.

(dissonance)

Elemental traces of soul
collide and smear upon the same.

Isotopes adrift and apart
in this atomic dream.

Masses moving through the rigors
of microcosmic space.

The exchange of thoughts the
traffic of nucleus and you.

I wish for sleep in the
hyperactivity of reasoning.

Such futility in wishing.

I hinge upon the light that shafts my mind
and detonate without regret.

(manhattan)

We were bereft from the world.
Cast as stones from sullied hands.
That dance you and I aspired
was just Psyche taunting her soul.
I knew as one always knows
when baring oneself to your hail.
It was so. These wings alighting
on your soil. Native earth
foreign to the touch yet
welcome to these eyes.
I spied you from a perch
long held dear.
From a vantage aloof to despair.
In swooping, I fell.
Dashing myself. Breaking my ire.
Finding sharp corners grinding
against the hard tang of
my denial. Now I know.
In flying and falling,
what most I desired from a distance.
What I disdained close to you.
That, my love, and times hence
is something true.

(unlikely you)

Escher spires in the dusk.
flowing in and back and up.
architecture that must
make me mad
with
this endless toil
of finding reason.

like finding you.

syncopated you.

predestination is a skullcap to creativity.
and I've created you
strand by wispy strand.

a route of mimicry.
I am a creature like you.
Wilde told me to say so
for the sake of art-
decadence in our need
to pander beyond
convention.

wider than the mock seas we have
placed between and before us.

hushed in the lining of our
need for old
nouveau.

this beauty in defiance
of truth.

(corinthian)

Skewed we were skittish.
I needed perspective.
Something I lost in
moments engaged with you.
I needed your soul. To tell me I found
a bit of myself at last.
So, it's true.
These moments I cherish.
A man. Glimpsing you from afar.
A woman. In her looking glass.
Who are you?
Ofttimes, it was me, falling.
Peering, as if demure; rising, as
if I knew.
Let me touch your rune.
That hazy portal beheld by
those we scorned.
As a pensive man, shorned.
As a woman, adorned.

(projection)

It was never easy. Those easy soliloquies
made to appease the easiest parts of myself.
Truth be told. In every fold of easy wit
underlying the folded pleats of your skirt.
These were the verses of our lives.
The uneasy pleasure of your flesh pressed
with measure upon my protraction.
I protest. You laugh. A smile breaks between us.
An exacting of what we reckon to be.
You seize the day and I the moment.
I breathe as
you leave.

(latter day)

When my unusual became routine.
And they came as dew to the
morning petals. As noon when
the markets settle.
Coy, the ever shifting focus of
millennial streams. The eclectic
dreams that we chase in never
ending stupor we deem.
When these ripples, purposeful
and willful, seep into my
pulse like an impatient
sculptor. That grace, that in
generations wane, will wax
when, ever hopeful, I see
you in an ever after.

(a priori)

Might trees be given slower speech
Than that which blood possesses in
A manner human and of flesh.
Yet the soul of wood does manifest,
Mature and strong, a sublime effect.
For such ambition runs deep in
All beings reaching and finding,
Inexorably, the far sky.

(mystic cellulose)

Inconstant, your definition bends.
My Lord. Your eyes. So brown. Condescends
My will and breaks my reverie. How?
I ask and why do I just now
Upon such revelation chance on.

The bird is dead. My thoughts like white bread.
I said before, "My soul can be read."
To those with interest in context.
Let not the outer form so vex.
My grave for you to dance upon.

(coquette)

we swim in the dim
of hallowed settings.

the sun has run and
the argo moorings
are no longer needed.

stiff iron –
the ferris wheel
of lacquered seals
on equine heels.

round and round, we laugh.
did you want the buggy?
the idle shoe?
the circular path so lovely
in gold, green, and
blue.

let me kiss you with my eyes.
my lips will not reach from
here – from the
white horse.

no, your mermaid body,
run through by a carnival
spear, is just as quick
as my trusty steed.
need will not close
the gap.
we believe in running,
in circling, in cycles
attuned by fancy.

we believe in the brush and pen –
stabbing ourselves with art.

up and down and again.

if you knew how my white horse
thrilled at the chase.
wooden sinew with a soul

carved from that which
made us all.
your laugh blinds you.

(carousel)

Stucco on my wall make imprints.
Heady.
Hold steady, my love.
You move like a charm that finds my will -
Too quickly.
Spinstress of Dionysus.

Let us go.
The retreats of our virility.
The haunts of our youth.
Prufrock would mock our appeal for love.
Our call to this.
This contradiction in our breath.
This spatial relation between wit and tone.
Must I groan in moments like this?
Despair over the fleeting notion of this?

Hold a bit and take a bit.
Your teeth bridge my tongue -
Hold my next act and find my reason.
Weep as we go.
Hold steady, my love.
Stucco on my ceiling is an engram of you.

(anamnesis)

Two years pass.
Rocked round the surly wraith
of your embrace.
These moments set
my neurons apace.
Leaves my resolve agape.
Were it not for shame.
A penchant for grace.
Would I pen these
nocturnal thoughts for
rhetoric's sake?
Under the moonlit guile
of this evening's break,
romps the remains of
our ruse… gathered willfully
against our bosoms in
reflection's wake.
The high rise horizon
of our modern vista,
bathed in neon necessity,
calls to me as you
once did.
Resplendent and free.

(kowloon)

The city is blue
according to you.

Try as some will.
Think as some are wont.

A town like this is full
of the clinically sane.

Ten blinks of Nystagmus
And I find that the rotation
of the world is inconstant.
A reflex from
loving you like this.

The sky is blue
for me.

I have nothing to lose.
I choose my fatalism
without
a clue.
If I knew, but I do.
It is still you.

Place a bit of me
easy on your hips
as you take the
curl from my tongue –
Claiming that the
World is a folded
Piece of origami.

Side to side.

I had to kiss you
For the salvation
Of your insanity.

The moment is blue.

I enjoy the slow tease

Of making us a habit.

The indescribable tango
Of ambition and obsession.

Your smirk in midst of it all.

How blue this city can be.

(molly)

Goose, Macallan, Tanqueray Ten.

I used to love drinking and cling restless on this wagon.

I just have to say I wish I knew you. How easily distracted when caught in my own reflection. When reaching out I admire the angle to shape of my own hand while missing to hold yours. There's more I'm sure. Less of me is what should be but I can't but feel a short contraction in my reverie. That up and down and round about to myself. Being observed and observing the skein of my feelings woven into yours. I love to be in love, and that inevitable invertibility makes me fall out of love. I used to think that was cool. Now I'm not so sure. If I were to pass a thousand souls, carelessly and casually, on these forgotten streets, would I even know it was you?

(chiasmus)

My hubris. Your egress. Echoes of
the pride before the slip.
As the world fell around our
walls. Brick by baleful brick.
The contention of our world
so nihilistic - bent on consumption.
In retracing, we fumble.
The ratios of indices
mumbling the jumbo open and
tremulous close of vestings
shrill to the quiet sentiment
of our prose.
Love - a relic we stow in boxes
both secular and modular.
Us - a vintage coupling with
the intention of something better.

(discount theory)

Time traveling I lost you.
Discordant, concentric skipping.
Sipping slowly I saw you.
Trapped in your plane of view.
Reaching out I missed you.
As though another held you.
These delta dreams mock me.
Free of waking reasoning.
The gravity of my pining.
Bending my course of travel.
Dilating, my heart unravels.
These coarse strands of us.
Our impossible paradox dust.
It was the past I adored.
The tomorrows I strove for.
Faring these lines of time.
You were only briefly mine.
Time traveling I lost you.

(relativity)

why would the stills of you
still mock me? i was looking
out through mahogany frames
made inane by the candor
of our tree.
maples spiral from time
to time and we begin
on cycles bred by long lapses
into the sublime.
taking slow reach. we
find some comfort in sleep.
we find a little infinity
amidst our fall.
keats we kin. we marry shelley.
where have you been?
drying high on some
seam made mad by insomniac
stitching?

i was looking for you. wanted
to tell you about the stars
before they go. the night
under her lazy robe.
so beautiful.
the satin and still, the little
cotton balls trimming the urban
pillow. how we sleep and dream
the last of jealous dawn away.
til last night makes a small
echo in our waking breaths.
so beautiful.
the afterglow. the first
kiss hello. the slow roll
of california. tell me you
know of this. my letters for
every sigh, for every place we lie.
i wanted you to know that
not everything was careless
design. that the moment
walks with me ever.

(fin)

originals

If I took a little time
Selfishly for my own
to do what hearts like mine
are prone to do when every line
traces itself to you.
A bit of time to breathe
Suddenly on my own —
to know this breath of mine
Slow and sure, is a quantum
entangled with yours —
As if for the first time.
Achingly new. Deliberately unknown.
To brave this world of ours,
Spinning callously amongst the stars,
together with you...

Good evening, love —

I tried to forget all about you.
Your steps traced on synaptic scars
pick stitched by what seems to be
memories of you.
It was neural yet static.
The cleft the same but a leap astute.
These hurdles in my head
a lonesome goal to you.
I am iota.
Struggling to cross the membrane
bound in regret of you.
To escape into inhibition
that I might, excited and frantic,
be pruned into insensate reflection of you.
I am through.
Changing in a flood of change
washing away from you.
To find a state free and easy
A place torpid - no longer pedantic
I tried to forget all about you.

It was very likely true
Being mad about You.
But you are just that.
And very likely more.
those brazen days you and I
sculpted the sky from the
whispers between our lips.
these dreams of you and I
slipping free of the venus
bound in between your hips.
this fury of desire only
coded by the embrace of
your thighs.
I was not mad at you.
Just that you confound me.
Enveloped in confusion.
As I find clarity in coming.
You are so very likely.
Fuck you

Time traveling I lost you.
Dischordant, concentric skipping.
Sipping slowly I saw you.
Trapped in your plane of view.
Reaching out I missed you.
As though another held you.
These delta dreams mock me.
Free of waking reasoning
the gravity of my pining.
Bending my course of travel.
Dilating, my heart unravels.
These coarse strands of us.
Our impossible paradox dust.
It was the past I adored.
The tommorows I strove for.
Facing these lines of time.
You were only briefly mine.
Time traveling I lost you.

—His   7/26/17

Regal 170/20,21

Your chair across the dining
table sat empty;
A reminder ~~that~~, our hearts, like
my appetite ~~was~~ arbitrary
These days of ours, given to fancy,
cast over and through the net, like
currency ~~virtualized~~ for the sake of economy.

Saying I missed you would be ~~faux pas~~;
~~In the~~ sense that we all have ~~forgotten~~ art.
The old gods have fallen.
~~Something~~, in living ~~today~~, we knew.
Our ~~inbox~~, relentlessly, keeps calling.
The likes, and dislikes; we eschew
That, in living, we embolden—

Surely, my kind is dying if not dead.
My pen, in strokes like recursive computing,
is extant in metaphor only;
When we lament our missed meetings
as if our attempts at buying an alarm
ringing — gave meaning to centurning.
~~Booting~~ the need from which we were bred.

We were bereft from the world.
Cast as stones from sullied hands.
that dance you and I aspired.
was just Psyche taunting her soul.
I knew as one always knows
when tearing oneself from your hail.
It was so. these wings alighting
on your soil. Native earth
foreign to the touch yet
welcome to these eyes.
I spied you from a perch
long held dear.
From a vantage aloof to despair.
In swooping, I fell.
Dashing myself. Breaking my ire.
Finding sharp corners grinding
against the hard tang of
my denial. Now I know.
In flying and falling,
what most I desired from a distance.
What I disdained close to you.
that, my love, and times hence
is something true.

Those quiet trees in our range murmur
A lament to those requiems we utter
when passing solemnly under the
shade cast by our favorite maple.
Remembering the spring we shared
by the brook where we cast stones
too light with our laughter into
the ponds of our copse easy with
the smiles of summer's ripples
Your dappled coat. My wool scarf.
Those accoutrements we saved for fall.
That we might, to playfully spite,
the bronze days before old man's winter
Frosting the air between us with
the breath of shared desire.
A longing for ever.
And when again I walk this glen.
I swear, I live the moment with you as then.

So we spent, you and I.
Above ourselves, under the sky
So we take our last leave.
No lines to pine.
You say dismissal my reprieve.
From that which we turn
and cease never to see.
That lilt in breath that
takes us eagerly.
Freely I loved, openly I
grieved. That from the
earth we all receive.
The pen in my intent.
Ever mocking what
could have been.

there had to be You.
In that trace I swallow-laugh.
This moment after that I
savor and lament.
Those times before we spy
with instruments meant for
dissent.
On this pond. This small body
that I lay.
This last time I pen in
hopes to find you again
The beginning of another strand.
Another start. And I still
think of us in a land
where our home may stand.

When my unusual became routine.
And they came as dew to the
morning petals to noon when
the markets settle.

Coy, the ever shifting focus of
millennial streams. The electric
dreams that we chose in never
ending stupor we deem.
When these ripples, purposeful
and willfull, seep into my
pulse like an impatient
sculptor. That grace, that in
generations wane, will wax
when, ever hopeful, I see
you in an ever after.

11/24/18
#1604

Appendix: Chronology

Notes & One Endnote

Cypress and Among The Willows (or versions thereof) were published, I believe, by the Poetry Foundation in some coffee table album that I did not buy - most likely because the twenty-something me thought I should have gotten a free copy for giving them a free poem.

These poems are published with little, if any, subsequent edits, including letter case, whether it was penned or by keyboard input. Much of my work is unchanged from the penned versions as those found in the "originals" section. It is such joy writing with pens even as I sometimes misspell words under a cantrip of Grey Goose.

Practically all the poems had a muse for its intended destination, and they are as the day I wrote them. To this day, would that I could, I would.

This short book of poetry is divided into three sections with the absurdism of the clown dividing love and the strands of being within oneself. The poetry is sorted into these three sections based on sentiment rather than chronology. The titles are parenthetical afterthoughts. The poems always came first. They echo the idealism of the spirit of the age that we should fight to keep. This rumination is more pronounced seeing the span of nearly a decade when I wrote no poetry. A time, perhaps, necessary to empirically feel the world with its layers of philosophy, socioeconomics, nature, science, ambition, negligence, preponderance among nations and raison d'être. That true liberty is the most sacred right. Absurd, yet most profoundly, poetry was a part of all of it. Live free...

----

[1] Tiffany Wouters, "Love...Love Will Keep Us Together," A hotmail email, 2000

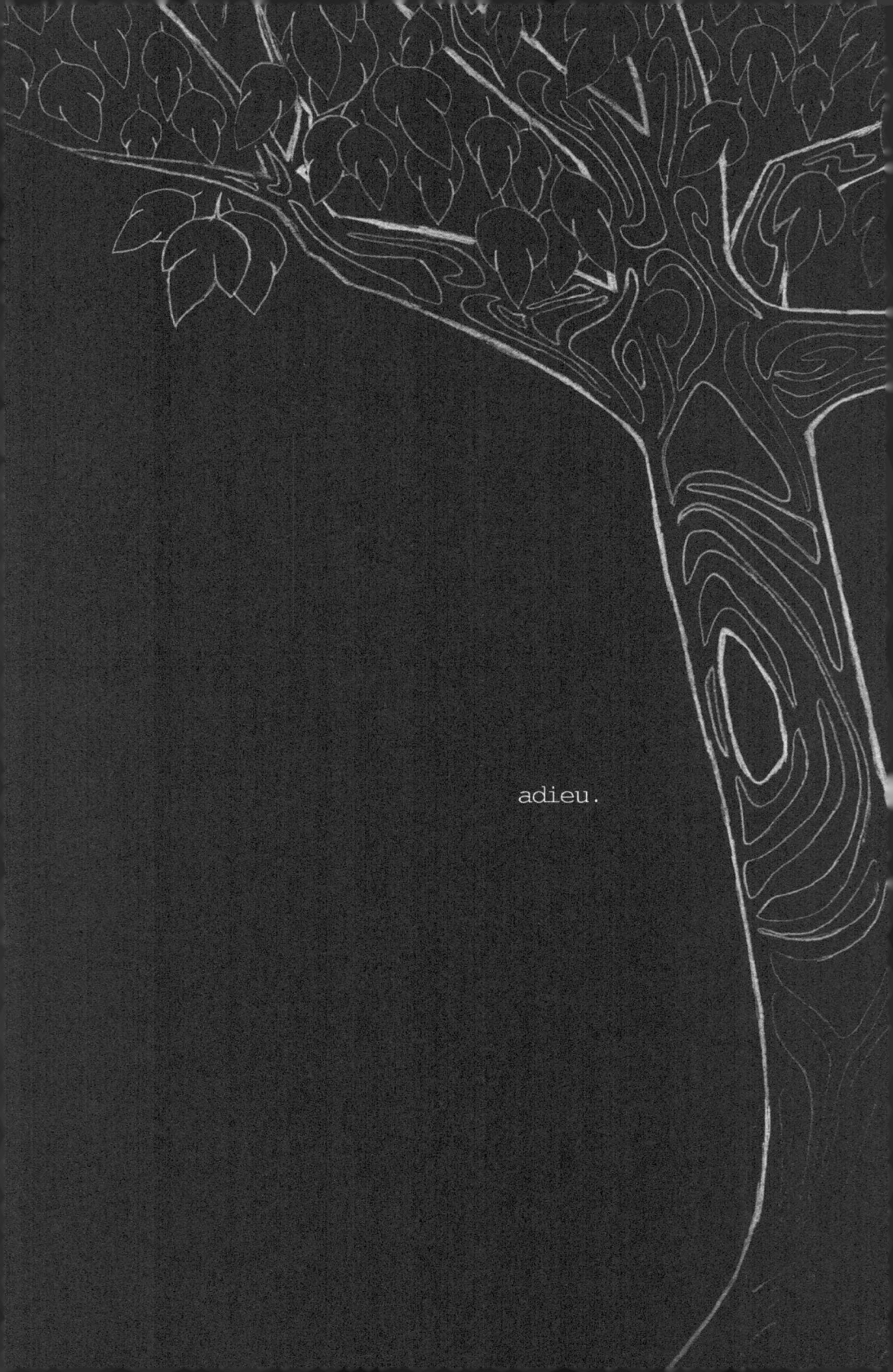

adieu.